D1027439

CHIVAL

BE A PRINCE. NOT AN INVADER.

BY

TOMMY WOOD

BRETT!

BE CHIVAL...

AtlasNovella Publishing (a division of Terebinth Tree, Inc.)
Jefferson, Georgia 30549

Copyright ©2022 Thomas Wood, Jr.

All rights reserved. No part of this book my be reproduced or transmitted in any form or by any means, electronical or mechanical, including photocopying, recording, or by any information storage and retrieval system, without the written permission of the author, exept where permitted by law. For permissions, contact: tommy@bechival.com

Edited by Stephanie M. Wood
Cover Art Woodcut byAlbrect Dürer - 1513
"Knight, Death and The Devil"
Cover Design and Interior Design by Tommy Wood

Publisher's Cataloging-in-Publication data

Names: Wood, Tommy, 1970-, author. | Wood, Stephanie M., editor.
Title: CHIVAL : be a prince. Not an invader / by Tommy Wood; edited by Stephanie Wood.
Description: Includes index. | Jefferson, GA: AtlasNovella (a division of Terebinth Tree, Inc.), 2022.
Identifiers: LCCN: 2022946881 | ISBN: 979-8-9870147-0-7 (paperback) | 979-8-9870147-1-4 (ebook)
Subjects: LCSH Men--Conduct of life. | Masculinity. | Man-woman relationships. | Self-realization. | Self-actualization (Psychology). | Self help. | BISAC SELF-HELP / Personal Growth / General
Classification: LCC HQ1090 .W66 2022 | DDC 305.31--dc23

ISBN: 979-8-9870147-0-7

This book is dedicated to...

Thomas Leon Wood, Sr
The Knight who taught me to joust.

Thomas Leon Wood, III
The Squire entrusted me by the King.

Stephanie Wood
The Queen who holds my heart.

Sofie & Selma Wood
The Princesses deserving of Princes.

The King
Who rules all.

(and to Albrect Dürer... because he rocks)

Table of Contents

"If you need to know the measure of a man, you simply count his friends."
- Paul Williams

Taken from the lyrics to Thankful Heart from The Muppet Christmas Carol.

In Chival, Tommy Wood teaches us a moral and social code forged by 10th century knights, which many have forgotten. In his writing, we learn to treat all with respect and hold ourselves to a higher standard. With the world's drastic decline of morality and increase in fatherless homes, this book gives a guide for us to learn and pass down for generations to come.

As Tommy Wood's son, I was fortunate enough to grow up with this code instilled in me. Because of this, I've always found it easy to be chival. I've found myself holding the door for my friends' girlfriends before, after their boyfriend left us behind. Little things like that may seem trivial, but as Eric Draven said, "Believe me. Nothing is trivial."

When I proposed to my wife, her roommate posted "I love these two so much, and they've shown me what a relationship should look like." This made me happy as it was a statement I was used to hearing about my parents. My dad often says he's made many mistakes, but if there's one thing he's done right, it's his family. His love for my mom is profound, and anyone who knows them sees it. I'm grateful to have grown up surrounded by that love. If that's the kind of relationship you're looking for, this book will get you there.

- Tré Wood

THE KNIGHT
WHO TAUGHT ME TO JOUST

One day when I was about five years old, I went to work with my dad. I always liked spending time with him at the office, plus I could usually score a glass bottle of Sprite out of an old-school vending machine. This particular vending machine looked like it came straight out of the fifties and had a narrow refrigerator door that opened after paying. You had to pull that freezing bottle out by the sharp metal cap. It was a special kind of pain but worth it. That transparent green bottle with those embossed bubbles was like a jade treasure that was all mine. I've got a thing for colored glass.

My dad owned the second equipment rental store in the Atlanta metro area, and he was well-connected in the city. That particular day we were headed to the bank, and he told me that the bank president would offer to shake my hand. He said I should take the banker's hand right away and shake it with a firm grip. Nobody likes to grab a cold floppy fish. We hopped in my dad's truck, and he drove us to the bank. As we walked in, I prepared for my moment. The banker greeted my dad with a big smile. They shook hands, and I was next. It happened just as my dad said it would, and I had taken one more step into the world of being a man.

My father taught me the importance of relationship and how to represent myself well. His guidance on things like how to treat women, when to give generously and when to stand my ground are just fractions of the instinct he instilled in me. Dad reinforced what he knew to be true by relating his past to my now. He showed me through his words and his actions how to make the best lasting impression. Leon Wood was a tough guy with an even tougher father of his own. One time, when I was sassy, he told me how his father would have thrown him across the tennis court if he had said what I said. I guess he learned what not to do from his dad as well - the hard way. But, in the midst of it all, my dad was compassionate and tempered himself down a few notches from what his experience had been. Even under that hardened exterior, he was also a man of grace. Once after I hurt my pride by nearly taking out the television with my brand new set of free weights, he sat by my side and put his arm around me. No words were needed.

Now, my mother also has a lot to do with me being who I am today. Her altruistic heart made a big impact on me. She loved me unconditionally, even though sometimes she tried to change the conditions. She only popped me with a flyswatter once. And, I deserved it.

It's important to have the balance of solid faithful male and female influences in our lives - at all stages. As I shared at his funeral… if I am a good father, it is because of him. If I am a good husband, friend, boss or brother… it's because of Thomas Leon Wood, Sr.

Here's to you, Dad.

WHAT IS OUR ROLE AS A MAN?
STRENGTH, LEADERSHIP, POWER, AUTHORITY, GUIDANCE, PATIENCE...

ARE GOD'S GIFT TO US AS MEN. WE HAVE TO CHERISH THAT, NOT ABUSE IT... I HOPE THAT THE WORDS IN MY MOUTH AND THE MEDITATION OF MY HEART ARE PLEASING IN GOD'S SIGHT.

- DENZEL WASHINGTON

Photo courtesty of A24 Films LLC / The Tragedy of MacBeth

CHIVARY
INTRODUCED US TO THE LEGEND OF
KING ARTHUR
THE ONE MAN IN MANY, WORTHY TO PULL THE
SWORD FROM THE STONE. A MAN OF EXCEPTION,
NOT THE RULE, KING ARTHUR'S LEGACY PORTRAYS
A REPUTATION WORTHY TO MODEL."

- TOMMY WOOD

Chapter One
A CHIVAL LIFE

Once upon a time, there was a code made by just and noble men. A code of knights, heroes and horsemen that adhered to the highest levels of social, moral and spiritual values. CHIVALRY. Born of the qualities expected in an ideal man, chivalry is a lifestyle of honor, courtesy, generosity, bravery, justice and readiness.

This once gallant revolution dared to combine a warrior ethos with courtly manners. Refined strapping dudes in touch with their emotions - sounds like every girl's dream, right? Though chivalry had its basis in knighthood, kings and nobility, through the centuries it grew to represent those same great qualities in the life of any man regardless of how many dragons he's slain.

It's important to keep telling the stories of both heroic dragon-slayers and the humble blacksmith. Those who keep their moral compass at hand and set a level plumb line build a firm foundation for future generations. One such story crafted during the birth of chivalry is *Erec and Enide*. Written by Chrétien de Troyes early in the twelfth century, this chivalrous romance cautions against a knight neglecting his chivalric duties. A young knight named Erec is so smitten by the love of his wife Enide, that he cannot seem to tear himself away from his marriage bed. Intoxicated by Enide's presence, he totally drops the ball on his military responsibilities. Too occupied to go and fight as a good knight should, Erec loses his reputation and even the respect of his wife. Finally, he gets his head on straight and undertakes a series of adventures to regain what he has lost - his prowess as a knight and the love of his wife. Spoiler Alert: In the end, Erec finds the right balance in his life between his role as a knight and his devotion to his beloved.

Chival is the title of this book though "chival" is not a word. It's a bit of shorthand that spontaneously appeared in my relationship with my own son. As he was growing up, I would teach him little things like opening a door for a lady or letting his sister go first when standing in line for ice cream. He would encounter some new scenario and recognize what he should do to be chivalrous. It came to be that I wouldn't even have to mention it. He would just do something kind or selfless for someone else and then turn to me and say, "Was that chival, dad? Am I being chival?" In childhood, an aspiring knight would emulate his favorite heroes - seeking to enroll his name in the chronicles of his own day. In similar fashion, my son was learning by example. Even though Batman and Han Solo are awesome, it's vital that the next generation has an affinity for the hero in the next room. As we age into knighthood, our valor and virtue become our story.

Chival instantly became a word at my house, and the spark of the idea for this book ignited. This chivalrous perspective dovetailed nicely with an issue that has plagued my heart for some time – the lack of fathering in our modern world and the subsequent fall and surrender of manhood. I don't mean to paint with too broad a brush. Thankfully, there are always exceptions. However, the daddy decay in the past five decades has reared its head as one ugly beast. Absent fathers, whether they live with their children or not, create a broken emptiness that compounds in a myriad of ways through the years. Guys, we must take responsibility and be courageous in our roles. We must also give place to our strengths and own up to our weaknesses. We have to look the beast in the mouth, and despite its bloody teeth and fiery breath, defend what is right and true. We owe it to those in our care to embody our prowess as both the king of our castle and a knight in shining armor. It is my hope, that by understanding and applying the ideals of chivalry to our modern lives, both younger and elder men can defeat the darkness and heal the damage born of this abiding affliction. That is a dragon we must face.

Chivalry became a great force in the Middle Ages, exemplifying the passion of the period. It revealed how the circumstances of a life could be raised from a base existence to a higher spiritual plane. Chivalry was largely an ideal. As no man is without sin, many failed to achieve their full aim. Yet even with all their faults, these pioneers of the code deserve great respect for their effort, which created a profound distance between them and the barbarism of the day.

The word chivalry was derived from the French word chevalier, which comes from the word cheval meaning horse Evoking the idea of a savior on a noble steed, the concept of chivalry was established to reduce the growing culture of violence and social distortion in their lands. When society fails to adhere, morals and traditions easily erode and decay over time. There's just an imprint of what used to be - relegated to museums and historical documentaries.

Some say chivalry is dead. Birthed in the twelfth century, it must be so old it has all but turned to dust, a fossil of a bygone age. But valor, courage, heroism and kindness do not go out of style. They are not skeletons on an ancient battlefield. These truths, these righteous bones, do not crumble into obscurity. No, I say that the knight's code lives.

We see it every day. Whether it's the EMT saving lives or a gentlemen giving his seat to someone who needs it, there is muscle and skin still living on this chivalrous frame. The evidence of chivalry is known in both large and small ways - through daring rescues or even the kindest nuance of a compliment. The awareness of our impact on the world around us is the blood in the veins of a modern warrior.

One might say that the chivalrous mantra should be... "I will do good. No matter what."

No one is perfect. Mistakes? I've made a few. I have launched into so many business concepts and failed so many times that one of my good friends said, "My wife would have left me by now." But that in and of itself is a testament to my chivalrous life. (Not to pat myself on the back or toot my own horn.) It's just that, even in debt and the disgrace of an unsuccessful business venture, my wife, my kids... they stood by me. Did my wife stay with me because I opened her car door or took out the trash? No. She stood by me because she knows my heart is hers, and my aim is true, even when I missed the target. Chivalry is a way of life. You see, even when I have failed to achieve some goal I pursued, the manner in which I loved, lead and protected my family has produced lasting relational dividends a millionfold.

Living within this ideology is not just about the tenants of chivalry, but it's a good place to start. To be chivalrous is a manner of being. With knightly skill and dedication, let us men show loyalty, self-control, hardiness, boldness,

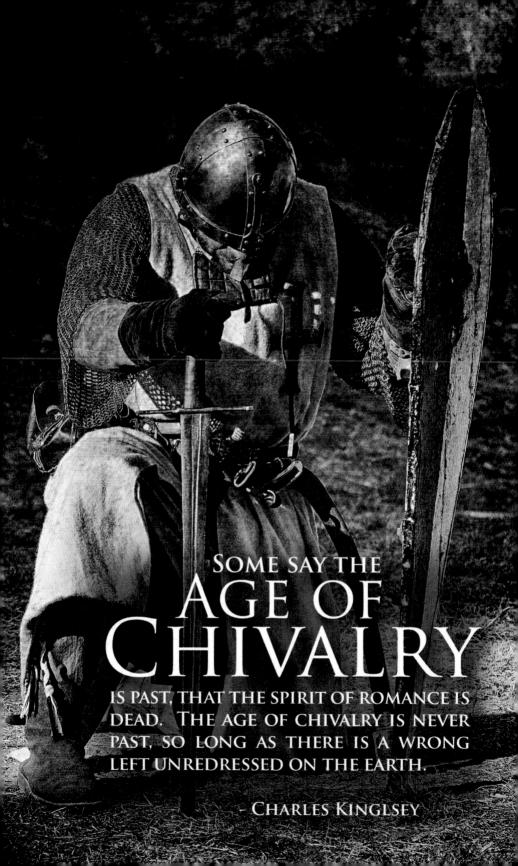

SOME SAY THE
AGE OF
CHIVALRY
IS PAST, THAT THE SPIRIT OF ROMANCE IS
DEAD. THE AGE OF CHIVALRY IS NEVER
PAST, SO LONG AS THERE IS A WRONG
LEFT UNREDRESSED ON THE EARTH.

- CHARLES KINGLSEY

THE TEN COMMANDMENTS
OF CHIVALRY

1 - HAVE FAITH & BE FAITHFUL
(NEVER COMPROMISE YOUR BELIEFS)

2 - DEFEND THE WEAK

3 - DEFEND YOUR COUNTRY

4 - TAKE TIME FOR SOLITUDE

5 - FORGIVE

6 - WORK HARD

7 - BE PATIENT. RESPECT OTHERS

8 - BE HONEST. NEVER LIE

9 - BE GENEROUS & GRACIOUS

10 - BE COURAGEOUS
(CHAMPION RIGHT & GOOD)

humility, dexterity, graciousness and love. Not fearing a sexist label, but knowing that our reputation proceeds us. A chivalrous man does not need to be a muscle-bound tough guy who's in touch with his feelings (though he can be). The key for any man of any size and age to live a chivalrous life is to put others first while remaining their steadfast guardian. It's about harnessing what is right and good and living within the habitation of that power every day. Don't be afraid of your masculinity. When tempered with the code, it is as strong as steel and never toxic.

The Ten Commandments of Chivalry were not written until 1883, at a time when some like Charles Dickens had already written Chivalry's eulogy. Here are the original ten.

THE ORIGINAL
TEN COMMANDMENTS OF CHIVALRY

- Thou shalt believe all that the Church teaches and thou shalt observe all its directions.
- Thou shalt defend the Church.
- Thou shalt respect all weaknesses, and shalt constitute thyself the defender of them.
- Thou shalt love the country in which thou wast born.
- Thou shalt not recoil before thine enemy.
- Thou shalt make war against the infidel without cessation and without mercy.
- Thou shalt perform scrupulously thy feudal duties if they are not contrary to the laws of God.
- Thou shalt never lie, and shalt remain faithful to thy pledged word.
- Thou shalt be generous and give largesses to everyone.
- Thou shalt be everywhere and always the champion of the Right and the Good against Injustice and Evil.

In order to streamline this list and re-imagine them for our modern times, I have rewritten the commandments in a simplified and more relevant way.

The Ten Commandments of Chivalry

- Be Faithful and Have Faith.
  (Never Compromise Your Beliefs.)
- Defend The Weak.
- Defend Your Country.
- Take Time for Solitude.
- Forgive.
- Work hard.
- Be Patient. Respect Others.
- Be Honest. Never Lie.
- Be Generous and Gracious.
- Be Courageous - a Champion of Right and Good.

We will discuss these commandments in more detail later.

We might not carry a physical sword and shield or ride on horseback these days, but we can evoke that same abiding resonance. When we walk into a room with our heads held high, our presence conveys our strength. People will hold for us that same respect and admiration that a warrior of old would have attained because they know who we are and we are a welcome sight. They know we are one of those men, who would fight on the front lines for the prosperity, hope and happiness of the whole. When people see you coming their way, give them reason to be glad.

Poets, minstrels and troubadours wrote and sang about the knights of valor. Geoffrey Chaucer was one such contemporary of the code. He lived and wrote when there were still real armored knights riding into battle and jousting in the tournaments. His concept of knighthood and chivalry is far more realistic than later authors looking back on that time with only stories to guide them. Chaucer's description shines a light on the true spirit of chivalry:

"There was a knight, a most distinguished man
Who from the day on which he first began
To ride abroad had followed chivalry,
Truth, honor, generousness and courtesy.
He had done nobly in his sovereign's war
And ridden into battle, no man more,
As well in Christian as in heathen places,
And ever honored for his noble graces …
He was of sovereign value in all eyes.
And though so much distinguished, he was wise
And in his bearing modest as a maid
He never yet a boorish thing had said
In all his life to any, come what might;
He was a true, a perfect gentle-knight.
Speaking of his equipment, he possessed
Fine horses, but he was not gaily dressed.
He wore a fustian tunic stained and dark
With smudges where his armour had left mark;
Just home from service, he had joined our ranks
To do his pilgrimage and render thanks."

Taken from *The Canterbury Tales,* trans. Nevill Coghill; New York, Penguin Books, 1951.

Chaucer examines the values that make up the Code of Chivalry. When called upon, the knight performs his brave duty valiantly. Yet even in his successes and renown, the knight is not a braggart - flaunting his wealth. Instead, he is generous and honest - not basking in his glory, but gracious in his success.

For now, we leave most historical references and flowery words behind. It's time to tackle chivalry in the modern age - to position ourselves for everything we want in the future. We're going to take a look at how a chivalrous perspective informs our choices. Let's take a look at what it means to be chival.

Chapter Two
DON'T BE STUPID

Don't make it how it shouldn't be. Do you get what I'm saying? Have you ever been in one of those situations where some guy just doesn't know when to shut up or maybe he's the only one who wore a marijuana-themed t-shirt to his sister's college graduation? Common sense and common courtesy should be a given, but let's bring it up a level. Be sensitive to those around you, and realize how your actions affect them and your environment. If you really want to elevate your persona, think before you act or speak, and don't be stupid.

All young men make mistakes. That's part of what growing up is all about. It's hard to figure out how to take your place in the world. Sometimes it can make you feel useless. What do we bring to the table? What are we good at? We are all flawed and inadequate. How do we learn to be articulate and shape ourselves into what we want to be? Will we find meaning and significance in our relationships, community, careers or heroism? How do we transform from a squire into a knight?

Maybe because I grew up with three sisters and no brother, I was keenly aware of their triggers, as in "girl" triggers. I have always had the reputation of being a bit more considerate than the average guy. That's not just my opinion; it is my experience. But, average is not what we are shooting for, right? We want to set ourselves apart in a way that attracts positive attention - not negative. Even if we ignore the thought, we long to be someone that someone else would want.

Typical marketing and entertainment are aimed at regular dudes - the median calculation based on focus groups and a dumbed-down version they are hoping to achieve. There is a ton of assumption and programming happening out there. Often, it's a very base, lowest common denominator approach. Hollywood and big corporations presume all males are just octane-fueled, sex-obsessed robots that want to shoot something. If you like the way that sounds, then you're a victim of their system. This indoctrination is a form of mind control. It has always been my goal to stand apart from the dumb masses who are slowly hypnotized into apathy. You may like *Grand Theft Auto* for its action and escapism, but a product like that is the antithesis of what it means to be chival, and it desensitizes you to the impact of your behavior in real life. We can't just press restart and get three more lives. Guys, we should not be so self-focused and unaware that we become couch-dwelling lumps high on Mountain Dew, playing video games, vaping blue-raspberry and smelling of Dorito farts. Nobody wants that. Trust me, the girl you want in your life doesn't want that in hers. And, don't get me started on "weed culture." I mean, come on. Do you want to smell like a frightened skunk and medicate your existence? Even if nobody else does, care about who you are and set a real course for your future. We should not rely on recreational drugs, alcohol or pharmaceuticals to keep us in check or cause us to check out. There's a psychosis out there called Mass Formation, and if you're not careful you can become the number this world wants to assign you… and not the man you are meant to be. I'm no NPC… how about you?

In Chapter One, I noted the hallmarks of a chivalrous man being noble, brave and all that. I thought it was interesting that Romans 1:31 gives a list that is quite contrary to that of a chivalrous man. I would call these the attributes of a non-chivalrous man - actually maybe even more of an evil man. The list describes these dark designations as unrighteousness, sexually immoral, wicked, covetous, malicious, envious, murderous, deceitful, backbiting, backstabbing, hater of God, violent, proud, boastful, disobedient, untrustworthy, unloving, unmerciful, and unforgiving. That's a pretty heavy list. You might say, "Murderous? I don't think so." However, we have to keep tabs even on our thoughts. You know how dark things cross your mind. It's not your fault, but it is your responsibility. We have to weed the garden of our lives in both our actions and internally. Little by little, we can remove the lies, the lusts and every notion that goes against what is good for us. I like to say, "We should go after not what is good for us but what is God for us."

Did you know sin is a term in archery? It means to miss the mark. An archer aiming at a target learns to control breathing and release. With time, coaching, and practice, higher and more dependable accuracy is achieved. I think we can learn a lot from that. We don't want to have a view that sin is only the evil that men do. Sin literally means missing the mark - to miss what you're aiming at and be off target. Take a moment. Reflect on yourself. Establish your goals. Practice makes perfect - or at least better.

I've only been in two fist fights in my life. Both of them involved playing tackle football with the neighborhood kids. In thinking back, I guess I picked both fights. I lost the first one and gave up on the second. In short, the first one was because a guy tackled me and made my brand new IZOD shirt do that ripping noise where you hear but don't see any damage. I still went after him. He was bigger. I was stupid. I lost. I bled. The second fight had a similar tackle-angered genesis, but when I jumped the guy from behind he just collapsed like a toddler who didn't want to be picked up. I felt so bad for even thinking about attacking this beefy guy that I just walked away in private shame. I say all this because (just ask my friends and family) I am an easy-going guy. However, I used to have a temper. I recognized that temper, and I had to tame that beast. Could I still blow up? Yes. I have. Still, I am a better man for having made the effort to be a better man.

One day at Chick-fil-a, I was sitting with my breakfast, my journal and my laptop. Four teenage boys came in and sat at a booth on the opposite wall. One of them fired up YouTube on his phone and proceeded to share a car chase complete with gunshots and profanity with the rest of the customers. Sounds like a typical day at Chick-fil-a, right? Kidding, of course. Just when you thought he was done, he would start up some other scene he thought was hilarious. It was very loud and distracting. As I was exchanging glances with everyone else, I was afraid of what these guys might watch next. No one could concentrate, and I finally had enough. I stood up and kindly but firmly asked the offender to consider what he was doing, and how it was affecting people like myself who were there to read or work. As people do when they are busted, he took offense. Everything from then on was sarcasm – from both of us actually. Whether right or wrong, my knee-jerk reaction was to give him some sass right back. Maybe not my most "chival" response, but you see how his self-centeredness created an environment that bred conflict. He was reaping the seed he was sowing in real-time. I wasn't ugly to the kid, just abrupt. Anyway, at least one of his friends

GUYS, WE CAN'T BE SO SELF-FOCUSED THAT WE BECOME

COUCH-DWELLING LUMPS

HIGH ON MOUNTAIN DEW,

PLAYING VIDEO GAMES,

VAPING STRAWBERRY-KIWI

AND SMELLING OF DORITO FARTS.

NOBODY WANTS THAT.

- TOMMY WOOD

It's easier
to build
STRONG
CHILDREN
than to
repair
BROKEN
MEN

-Fredrick Douglas

felt bad and was clearly embarrassed. That means only twenty-five percent of these guys seemed to know better. So, what's the solution? The instigator in all this should have waited to show his friends these videos once they were back home or sitting in the car. Why couldn't it wait? It totally could and should. It was not the place or time to revel in their guy-ness. I will concede that sometimes guys will be guys and need to be guys. It's a part of coming of age to goof around, find out things our parents are afraid to tell us, and lock horns with the other studs on the mountain. A little carefree bravado is not a bad thing. After all, learning to be a man who respects and considers his own semblance is also part of growing up. Sometimes our youth takes over, and we just want to show off. Understanding the time and place for things… well, that comes from experience and maturity. It's what you might call wisdom.

I was driving my kids to dinner one night. My wife had plans to hang with friends, so it was taco night with dad. As we were headed to eat at our favorite Mexican place, I was looking for a good song on the radio. The classic rock station was playing a Pink Floyd song. Even though my daughters were raised on hard rock and Weird Al parodies, Floyd is a bit more esoteric for their tastes, and they'd prefer a little Top 40 over 70's mind melt. I know this about them, so I found something they would like on the pop station - something I knew my son could tolerate. Right after I changed the station, my son asked, "Dad, do you not like Pink Floyd?" I told him I did, but I knew his sisters were probably wondering what the heck we were listening to, and I wanted to find something that everyone in the car would be cool with. It was a teaching moment that happened on its own. He saw that I was being sensitive to everyone around me, and I recognized that he was learning. Of course, there has been a time or two when

Van Halen came on and I turned it up without regard to my daughters' pop tendencies. It was because I knew I would be a goofball and get laughs playing air guitar or at least tell them the story behind my love for the band (part of their rock-n-roll education). They expect that from me at this point. Floyd is not what most girls born after 1990 want to hear on the way to get Mexican food. This story may only contain a small nuanced consideration of what it means to be chivalrous. Yet I believe even those small things are important.

In life, for men or women, it really all comes down to the golden rule. Treat others as you want them to treat you. You really do reap what you sow. For those not tuned in to farming metaphors, that means whatever seed you plant, that is the fruit you will get. It's a foundational truth in nature as well as in human relationships. If you sow discord, strife will find you. If you are kind, then kindness will be an attribute you are known for and kindness you should receive in return for your effort. If others still treat you poorly, you should take the high road. Shake it off, and move on. It will elevate your persona again and again. Your enemy will notice. Everyone will.

I met a guy. We'll call him Marcus. The MTSU t-shirt I was wearing sparked a conversation with Marcus, as I paid him for gas and a bag of ice. I learned that he had been a desired basketball recruit by MTSU and other schools, but after an injury and some poor choices, things did not turn out as he once had hoped. It was good to see that he took ownership of it all, but he did tell me how his parents were not in his life. That matters. I can't even describe how much that matters. Fortunately, Marcus had turned his vision in a different direction and was making music. He found out I was also a musician, and he asked what I do when it feels like nobody cares about what you're creating. Man, did I know where he was coming from. I gave him some encouragement and made sure to get back by to see him. Marcus is hungry to be relevant and to have relationships that shore up his heart. Without a father, Marcus was at a disadvantage. If we don't have the parents God gave us, He can and will provide more. We need guidance, and most of all we need love. If you're missing a father figure in your life, I encourage you to find one. Don't force it, just be looking out for it. A mentoring relationship with someone who has "been there and done that" is invaluable.

Approximately thirty percent of all American children are born into single-parent homes, and for the black community, that number is sixty-eight percent. According to David Blankenhorn, author of *Fatherless America*, America is "facing not just the loss of fathers, but also the erosion of the ideal of fatherhood." David Popenoe, writer of *The Decline of Fatherhood*, states, "The decline of fatherhood is one of the most basic, unexpected, and extraordinary social trends of our time... In just three decades, between 1960 and 1990, the percentage of U.S. children living apart from their biological fathers more than doubled, from 17 percent to 36 percent. By the turn of the century, nearly 50 percent of American children may be going to sleep each evening without being able to say good night to their dads." The U.S. Department of Justice reports that children from fatherless homes account for sixty-three percent of youth suicides, ninety percent of all homeless and runaway youths, seventy-one percent of all high school dropouts, and seventy percent of juveniles in state institutions. It's easy to see the holes that the absent father creates. Your circumstances do not have to be the proverbial baggage that weighs you down. If you find yourself at a disadvantage because your father has not been present in one way or another, you can reverse that curse from this day forward. It starts with making wise choices about who you want to be.

My father demonstrated to me how to shake a man's hand, when to put myself last and how to live as I want to be remembered. I've invested the same ideals into my son, and even some of his friends. Not everyone has that. To paraphrase the great movie A Knight's Tale, you can change your stars.

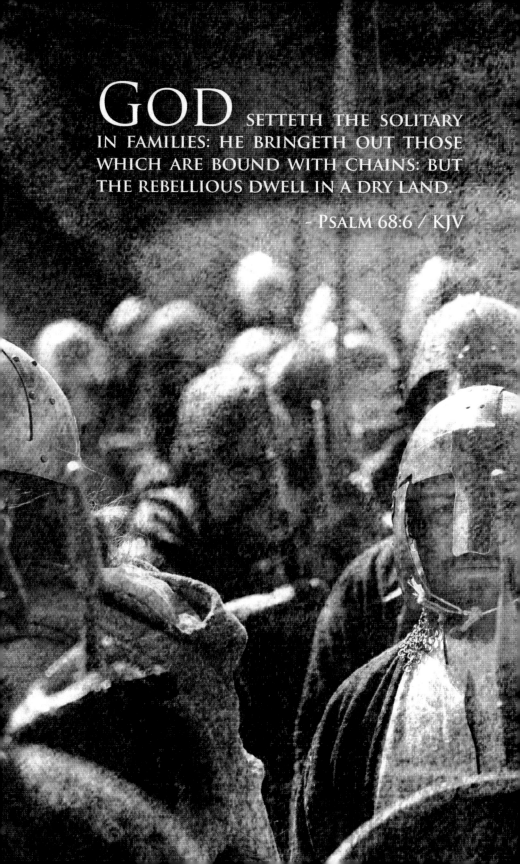

GOD SETTETH THE SOLITARY IN FAMILIES: HE BRINGETH OUT THOSE WHICH ARE BOUND WITH CHAINS: BUT THE REBELLIOUS DWELL IN A DRY LAND.

- PSALM 68:6 / KJV

IF YOU
BELIEVE
IN NOTHING ELSE, JUST
KEEP BELIEVING
IN YOURSELF.

- MYLES KENNEDY

Chapter Three
RESPECT IS NOT A 4 LETTER WORD

How are you remembered when you leave the room? Were they happy to see you or happy you left? What is your brand? Your image? Think of your life as a movie. What do you want to project on that giant silver screen for everyone to see? Are you the hero in that story? Or maybe the villain? Who do you want to be? Are you hiding something behind the scenes? Are you the same person alone as you are in a crowd or one on one? You should be. That's called integrity.

Our actions are our calling card. Our words are the breath of our memory. And respect is not a four-letter word. It's a seven-letter word. I jest, but my point is that there is power in what we say. When it comes to the lexicon of our daily lives, our word choice matters. Words are seeds. Words can heal, or they can wound. Words can paint a picture. In fact, they say a picture is worth a thousand of them. Words hold the power of life and death. It is good to think before you speak.

An actor friend of mine once wrote a blog stating that when he hits his thumb with a hammer, there are only certain words that will help him feel better. A specific one with a hard "k" is a favorite of his. I get that. Pain is an instigator. Whether we say it or think it, we're around enough cuss words in our daily life that they pop into in our brain automatically. If we say "dang" instead of "damn," are we really saying anything different? Another friend of mine posited, "Why is shit a bad word? That's what it is." Here's the thing and also the point of my friend's blog: We don't need to rely on colorful language to make us cool or tough. A moment of pain or passion might erupt in ways that might make our mothers frown, but peppering our conversation with scatologicals and f-bombs does not increase our intellectual prowess or cool factor. Sure, they are just words in the end, but words do have meaning, connotation and power. That's why people can be so offended by them. Be careful with words, not flippant. It means something visceral in our culture. If we don't want our toddlers running around dropping sentence enhancers on the general public, then in my humble opinion, we should tame our tongues. Listen, I've seen Jurassic Park. I know there are times when a single word ups the funny or drives the point more succinctly, but a mouth gushing with filth is not one most women want to kiss. Best to not leave that faucet running. If you have something significant to say, you don't need jagged words to cut through if your point is sharp enough. Let the content of your perspective leave the lasting impression.

Never shake a man's hand sitting down. This isn't just about respecting the other person; it's also about respecting yourself. It's about taking the time to do the things we don't do anymore, like standing when someone enters the room. One day I was pitching a screenplay at the Four Seasons in Beverly Hills. A few writers had gathered for a producer's lunch, and that day I had the opportunity to pitch a couple of my scripts to one of the producers of *Close Encounters of the Third Kind*. During our lunch, Morgan Freeman came over to meet us. Can you believe out of eight people sitting at that table (this includes the two producers), I was the only person to

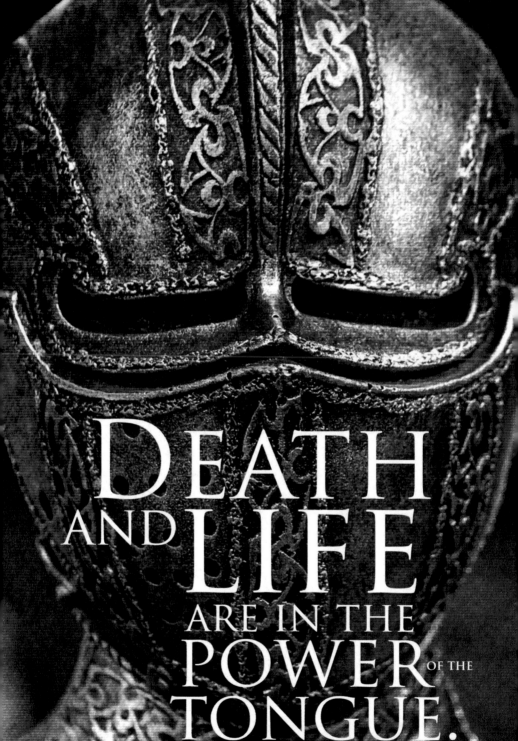

DEATH AND LIFE ARE IN THE POWER OF THE TONGUE.

— PROVERBS 18:21

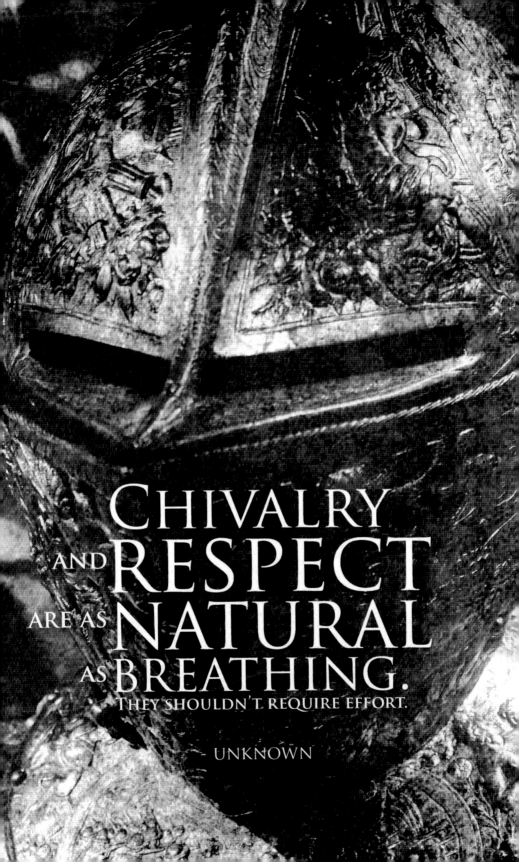

CHIVALRY
AND RESPECT
ARE AS NATURAL
AS BREATHING.
THEY SHOULDN'T REQUIRE EFFORT.

UNKNOWN

stand up and shake Morgan's hand? I was shocked. This isn't even about being chivalrous. He just happens to be one of the greatest actors of our time. And I'm the only person who stands to shake his hand? So who do you think Morgan might remember? I saw it in his eyes. He was surprised that I stood which is also a sad commentary on to what he had become accustomed. That was an opportunity I wasn't going to miss. Be ready. Stand out. Stand up. Respect yourself. Take time and embrace the moment.

Many years ago, I heard someone say that to love others you must first love yourself. Matthew 22:39 suggests that we should love others as we love ourselves. It makes sense that a perfect circle would be formed by loving and respecting our own lives and bodies, and in turn, treating others the same. There is power in what we believe and say about ourselves. Should we say things like, "My damn car is always in the shop?" Maybe it is better to say, "I'm glad my transmission is working again." It is best to speak life into our life - declare with your own voice who you are aiming to be and what your goals are.

When doing a job, do it right. In construction, they say to measure twice and cut once. That way you're less likely to screw up and waste lumber. Let's say you get a job, but you have to start out at the bottom. You're washing dishes. If you want to advance in your role at that job, be the best dishwasher you can be. Learn the trade and techniques for making your job more efficient. Arrive early. Most dishwashers quit after two weeks. If you do your best and apply yourself like you own the place, your actions will be noticed. In just two more weeks, you might be a line cook. In six months, you may be a shift manager. Whatever the job, see the big picture. Be the person you would want to hire if you did own the place.

To become a knight, a young boy around seven years old would start as a page in service to a knight. He would be given responsibilities like caring for the horses and maintaining armor. The boy would learn many skills from the knight, such as the mastery of horsemanship. Upon reaching the age of fourteen, the page would become a squire, which was basically an understudy to a knight. As squire, everything reached a new level where the growing young man would learn to master a variety of weapons and fighting techniques. At the age of twenty-one, the squire graduated to knighthood, pledging to the chivalrous code and being sworn into service in a sword ceremony. After the knight's dubbing, his father would say, "Go fair son be thou a valiant knight and courageous in the face of your enemy. Be true and upright that God may love thee."

When talking to my daughters about writing this book, one of the first things they brought up was appearance. Keep in mind guys... when I asked two young ladies (twenty-two and under) what to include in this book, the first thing they said was appearance. We can't all look like Zac Efron and Jason Momoa, but we can represent ourselves well. Over the years, I've heard that women judge us by our shoes. They might forgive a pair of cargo shorts or a wrinkled t-shirt as long as the shoes aren't disgusting. This note on appearance might not be a true tenant of chivalry, but consider the knight in shining armor. His shoes match his outfit - literally. I can't give you totally comprehensive shoe advice. You have to read the rooms that you frequent. Dirty, stepped-on, gross-looking shoes should be relegated to yard work. Get a decent pair of shoes. Even you frat boys.

Along with clothing and shoes comes hygiene. Brush your teeth. Clean up the facial hair. Put lotion on those

FOR AS HE
THINKETH
IN HIS HEART,
SO IS HE.
— PROVERBS 23:7

Boys are BORN, MEN ARE TRAINED.

- Jeffrey Prather

"dogs". I was probably thirty years old before I realized my feet didn't have to have dry and cracked areas. Presentation is an investment in acceptance, and acceptance gets you access. Whether it's a job interview or a date, look like you're ready for what's next. Take care of yourself, and don't get lazy. If you look good, it goes a long way towards feeling good and producing a confident swagger in your step.

Another point my daughters made about guys concerned their personalities. Hopefully, you have one. I'm sure you've heard that personality goes a long way... especially if you're not one those pretty boys. Personality carries a lot of weight. Sometimes pretty only goes skin deep. If you've ever taken a personality test or just did the online social media survey to see which Spongebob character you are, you've seen that we are all wired in different ways. For example, I'm more reserved. You may be the class clown who's ready for the party. I know I have been accused of being stuck-up because I didn't talk much. My daughters, however, think I am too quick to chime in on the ridiculous things in the world around me. I can be opinionated, but crazy is off the leash these days. Either way, I'm not about to force myself to be super outgoing. Like everything, balance is key. If I am too reserved, I might not stand up for myself or others when I should. I might not be heard. If I am too vocal, I may come off abrasive and lose the respect of others and maybe even friends. Self-editing is good as long as it doesn't neuter our passion. Depending on my personality type, I might have to be more forward... or maybe more reserved to be a balanced person. I might need to speak up or I might need to hold my tongue. In either case, be likable, even lovable. At a minimum, be respectable. Our individuality is our own. Make it what you want it to be.

An interesting point to add here: In the twelfth century, clerics created books called *Courtesy Books*. These books were intended to advise nobles on manners and personal behavior. Apparently, the elite of their day had to be told not to speak while eating due to the food that would fall from their mouths while talking. These books also suggested that the nobles not complain about the food that was given to them, stick their fingers in the mustard, or blow their noses on the tablecloth. One courtesy I found entertaining was their method for how to scratch your nose at dinner. Since most people ate from common platters and not individual plates as we do now, clean hands were imperative to not offend. The clerics suggested that, if your nose is itching, scratch it with a piece of bread and then eat the bread as opposed to scratching your nose with a finger and then grabbing food from the common bowls. These books were a nagging (and somewhat superficial) device attempting to reshape nobility. But hey, they weren't wrong. One final funny note on Courtesy Books, they were written in Latin and were largely inaccessible to nobles of the time, who probably couldn't read them anyway.

Our awareness of the world is also an important aspect to consider. Our great-grandfathers grew up reading the newspaper. Our grandfathers added television to that mix. Today, we are getting live-streamed opinions from across the world in real-time straight to the palm of our hands. Basic knowledge of what's happening is vital. Even better, dig in and educate yourself. A well-read individual can carry on a conversation with anyone. And let me recommend, go beyond the main-stream-media. They are controlled by huge corporations, and they all support the same narrative. Be an independent free thinker. Seek the truth, and spread it.

Age and experience are how some of us learn. We just can't listen when we are younger because we know absolutely everything, right? That being said, based on my age and experience, here are some extra fun thoughts on gaining respect.

- No peacocking in the free weights. Nobody cares.
- Squealing tires prove nothing.
- Beer is not a status symbol. You don't always need one.
- Act like you've been there before. Especially in the end zone.
- When entrusted with a secret, keep it.
- There are many ways to enter a pool. Don't take the stairs.
- Hold your heroes to a higher standard.
- Return a borrowed car with a full tank of gas.
- Be like a duck. Remain calm on the surface and paddle like crazy underneath.
- Never be afraid to ask out the best looking girl in the room.
- No cold fish handshakes.
- Don't be a ball hog. Pass it.
- Give credit. Take the blame.
- After writing an angry email or text, read it carefully. Then delete it.
- Eat lunch with the new kid.
- Try writing your own eulogy. Never stop revising it.

Chapter Four
HOW TO TREAT A WOMAN
IF YOU WANT TO LIVE

It has been said that men do not understand women. Men are like waffles and women are like spaghetti. A man thinks in blocks of information, and those segments of syrup do not intermingle, while a woman's brain is like a bowl of pasta where one noodle might touch sixteen others, and each of those, sixteen more. And if there's sauce on the pasta, look out! It's getting spicy! Ain't no telling which way that conversation is going. This is why my wife can ask me to put gas in her car, which reminds her that we have to attend a wedding out of state this fall, which reminds her that her grandfather used to own land in south Georgia.

Let's face it - the ladies have the upper hand. They mature faster. In general, they are not hard-wired to visuals (unless it's purses and shoes), and they are deeply connected to what they feel. Still, God made us male and female for balance. We need each other. We can even notice this balance in many of the most successful movies. When the male and female character arcs are both important and support each other, it makes the story work even better.

I've made the statement many times that "Guys are fifteen." What guys you may ask? All of them. Only the shell is aging. Hopefully, we mature and gain some wisdom over the years, but put a skateboard, fireworks or a pretty girl in front of just about any guy and his brain hits some gear that tells him he's a brand new Ferarri. As you grow up, just know that your internal self is the same guy with the same curiosities and dumb ideas that have always been there. Men are born wild at heart, and that's okay. That's who we are. Just know it's your job to reign in the beast inside.

We are not animals. We may be technically mammals, but we are not animals. As much as we humans love our dogs, they are beasts at heart. They scratch and lick with no care about who's around. They drag their butts across the carpet with no shame. Animals are driven by a primal notion to eat, sleep and find a partner in heat. Yes, I know your Golden Retriever is like one of the family, and he will cuddle and bring you a ball or maybe even a beer. He is still an animal that reasons by reward. An animal is out to satisfy its own desires. My little dog, Alice, loves to eat poop. Guys, don't be animals. We'll come back to this in a bit.

When interacting with women, whether they are girl-friend material or grandma material, we need to apply the chivalrous code. Listen to them. Listening gains you knowledge and perspective. Women don't necessarily ex-pect you to fix everything. Sometimes they just need you to hear them and share their pain. But, pay attention. Do not tune out. You might get asked a question, and boy you better be tracking.

It's not fine, and it's not nothing. If my wife says some-thing is fine, I probably need to dig a little deeper and find out what she really wants. If I ask her what's wrong and she says, "Nothing," it's probably something. I'm going to need to figure that out. At the same time, she could mean that something is fine and nothing really is nothing.

In which case, I better not keep asking because then I'm aggravating her and that's not fine... or nothing. That may sound complicated. Just pay attention. That's all.

There is a time and place to step in and get some boots off the high shelf, kill a spider, chase down a waiter, or snatch your wife back from an Islander who's trying to dance away with her at a Caribbean street party. Yes, I speak from experience. If you ever go to a Caribbean street party where the police have machine guns and the roads are lined with barbecue vendors, have fun and keep an eye out.

Opening doors can open doors. Let's say you take a cutie out on a date and the whole evening you're opening her car door and the door to the restaurant... you've made her the focal point. She knows she's special in your eyes. Don't let the complacency you see in other people's relationships cause you to drop the ball. It's worth the effort to go the extra mile. Compliment her. What is it about her that's making your heart beat faster? Be tasteful, of course. Give her your jacket if she's cold. By all means, don't check out other girls over her shoulder. Look her in the eyes. Men are wired to pursue, and women are wired to respond. Don't let that paradigm shift you into manipulating that relationship. You each hold powerful ground at each end of that spectrum.

If you see a damsel in distress, be careful. She might not be in distress, and she wants to work it out herself. If she pushes back at your assistance, don't take it personally. Move along. If you're meant to make a difference for her, you will.

Romance has taken a back seat to expediency and practicality. Sometimes, you need to go out of your way to affect her heart. If it makes her smile, do it more often.

Communication is key as they say. Be honest, but also be tactful. Be kind... always. Whether it's an important question or the unfortunate difficulty of breaking up, don't text her about it. Talk to her face to face. Embrace these moments of your life, even the tough ones. Be courageous. You'll be proud of yourself for engaging these moments with purpose. Take the high road no matter how hard the climb.

Speaking of the high road... I once knew a guy who did not act very chivalrous. It was me. I was dating a girl senior year of high school. The relationship started good, but it got weird. She was starting to hate anyone I had ever dated. We were starting to argue a lot over things in the past (a past that she was not even part of). I would like to take a sidebar here in defense of myself. My past relationships that angered her were not even serious. I was a good kid. Her perception of anyone but her in my life made her see red. One night, we were driving home from one of my rock band's concerts, and she started up. She complained that I didn't look at her enough from the stage and that led to yelling about the past again. Now, this part of the story probably gets into a relationship with a diagnosis of "unhealthy." What came next is where I failed. I was over it and basically over her. I was so sick of hearing all this that I erupted. In the flash of a nano-second, I weighed in my mind what lava I was going to spew. So, I did it. I yelled, "Stop acting like a B-word!" (I yelled the real word FYI. I did not abbreviate.) I knew things would go nuclear if I had yelled, "Stop being a B-word!" Because then, I would have been saying she was one... not just acting like one. But, I was so mad that I just had to say something, and I wanted to include that word for dramatic effect while limiting the emotional damage. My mistake. All she heard was the B-word. She slapped me across my face in such a way that I temporarily lost sight

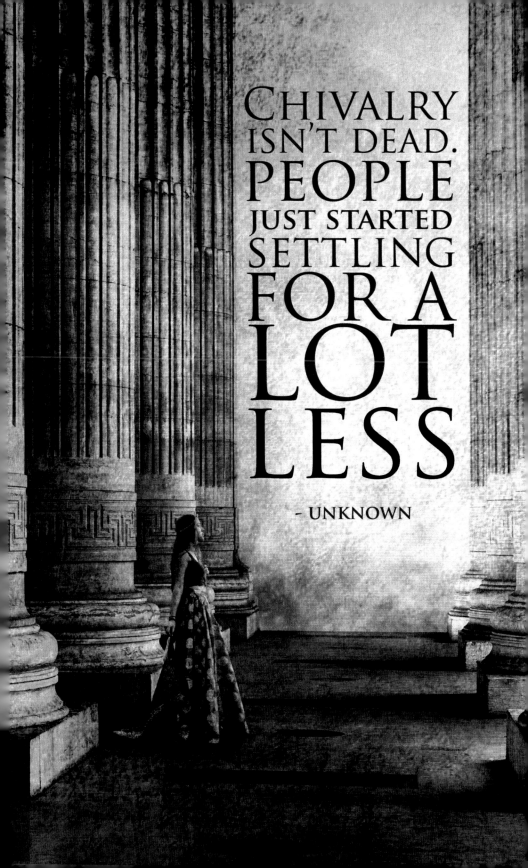

AN INTELLIGENT MAN WILL
OPEN YOUR
MIND.
A HANDSOME MAN WILL
OPEN YOUR
EYES.
A GENTLEMAN WILL
OPEN YOUR
HEART.
THE RIGHT MAN
WILL DO ALL THREE.

- UNKNOWN

in my right eye and had to pull over and wait until I could drive again. In summary, I should have taken the high road. Even if our relationship was basically dying, I really should have been the bigger man by keeping my mouth shut.

It's hard to say what would have been better in that situation, other than just saying nothing. So maybe sometimes… say nothing. Just take it, and if needed, find your escape plan. This is off-topic, sort of, but to the point of saying nothing: We can sometimes seem smarter when we say nothing. People perceive that we are thinking things through and have a strong opinion. When really, we just don't know what to say. As the old adage states, "It is better to be silent and thought a fool, than to open your mouth and remove all doubt."

Would I marry her? I think I asked myself this question for every girlfriend since Kindergarten. That first girlfriend when I was five was a pretty blonde. I gave her an Easter bunny ring. We never did get married though. In first grade, I had another blonde girlfriend (seeing a trend), and she kissed my cheek on the playground one day. She smelled like onions. I did not like that. Whether it was those girls or my next big crush which wasn't until fifth grade, I really did consider whether this was someone I could consider marrying. Even at a young age, I was thinking big picture. I encourage you to do the same. Could I have married that girl that slapped me silly? We talked about it. We dated for almost two years. But, no. She was not the one for me. There is nothing wrong with dating someone that's not right for you. You'll find out fast the kind of person you click with. Ironically, I married a brunette. Somewhere in college, I decided that aesthetic was really the direction I wanted to go. Just two weeks into dating her, there was a moment when looking into her eyes I realized she was the one. I hope one day you get that magic moment. Be patient. Speaking of being patient... I did not tell her that I knew she was the one at that point. That might have scared her off. I had to bide my time until I saw that she saw what I already knew.

One day, when you are in that moment and you do look into her eyes, ask yourself if you are enamored with the soul that's looking back at you. Or are you just liking how she's looking in those jeans? If you're not drawn in like the Millenium Falcon in a tractor beam, might be best to move on. She might be someone else's wife.

THE SINGLE ACT OF PAYING ATTENTION CAN TAKE YOU A LONG WAY.

- KEANU REEVES

WHAT YOU AIM AT
DETERMINES
WHAT
YOU SEE.

Chapter Five
DATING SOMEONE ELSE'S WIFE

What if you could be a fly on the wall when some guy is hitting on your wife, only this moment is five years before you've even met her? In this little fiction, you know she's your wife and with every move he makes you're ready to punch him. But, you're just a fly and he wouldn't even feel the impact of your tiny little fly hands. In fact, your buzzing would irritate him and he could squash you. Not only that, but he could actually emotionally hurt you because he got there first and did not respect you or your future wife. One day, you might feel squashed by that guy. A guy you never met - even worse if you do meet him. He could add unnecessary conflict between you and your wife months or years in the future by taking advantage of her in a moment of young lust. Again, it's the simple idea of treating others the way you want to be treated.

Ask yourself, "How do I want my wife to be when I find her?" If you want to find a person that has NOT been around the block a few times and just might be a virgin that saved that special moment for you, then treat everyone you date as if they are someone else's wife. They probably are.

We live at a time when some people don't think before they act. They often follow their primal instincts and wanton desires into destructive behavior. I'm always surprised when a young unmarried person finds themselves pregnant.

We all know what causes that. In our current culture, many would not consider intimate contact with someone with whom they are not married to be a bad idea. In fact for some guys, it's their primary goal. Maybe it's rebellion, wild oats or forbidden fruit. These days I would venture to say that most people have never been taught to consider the multi-faceted impact of sexual relationships. Every culture has its social and/or religious perspective on sex, but that is not the only aspect to consider. Remember me talking about taming the beast and not acting like animals? It's actually a bit psychopathic to be so impulsive that you are only out to satiate your sexual appetite. A self-centered, short-term, means-to-an-end action is shallow and narcissistic. Whether it be physical, emotional or spiritual there is always a price to pay. Obviously, there is the possibility of pregnancy and disease, but it's the broken heart that carries a devastation all its own. As much as people don't want to hear it, sex was designed for you and that special person to which you make a life-long commitment. It's a potent connection that we should not take lightly. We dilute the power of that relationship when we give pieces of ourselves away. To paraphrase Douglas Wilson: When a sexually active couple breaks up, basically what you have is a divorce without the legal fees.

People jump into sharing the sexual experience so quickly. You hear them say, "I wait until the third date at least." Of course, there are those that are up for an instant gratification social media booty call with the hope of no consequences. No offense, but that's ridiculous, dangerous and self-defeating. If you respect yourself and others, you won't treat sex in such a frivolous and selfish way. Saying NO right now, can result in a much better YES down the road. Don't give it all away. It's not a video game where you just hit reset.

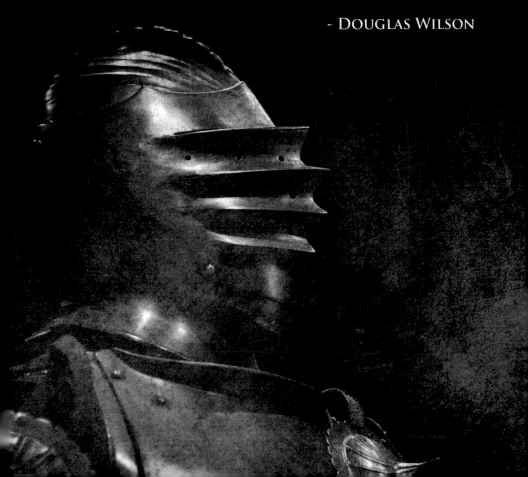

IF BOYS
DON'T
LEARN,
MEN
WON'T
KNOW.

- DOUGLAS WILSON

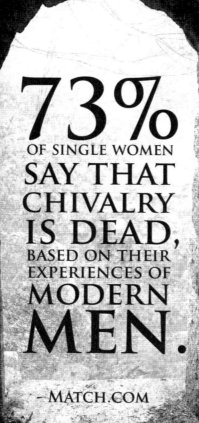

73% OF SINGLE WOMEN **SAY THAT CHIVALRY IS DEAD,** BASED ON THEIR EXPERIENCES OF **MODERN MEN.**

– MATCH.COM

One of the biggest problems a young man has growing up in the twenty-first century is pornography. Porn is fiction. Porn is poison. A porn addiction is prideful and selfish. It destroys your ability to have a healthy intimate relationship with your forever girl. Porn objectifies and dehumanizes people, while also fueling sexist attitudes. Consistent consumers of porn have a propensity toward violence in sex and are likely to struggle with impotence. It's a counterfeit intimacy with unrealistic expectations that creates real roadblocks to a happy marriage. When I was a kid, you had to try and score a dirty magazine or tweak out the cable box to get an X-rated movie. It wasn't the best use of our time, but sometimes that came from an innocent curiosity. Still, it all has the same roots that feed the same thorny weeds of the depravity we see so accessible today. Anything you can think of is available at your fingertips… likely for free at the end of a firehose. It's a dark dangerous road strewn with the wreckage of things you can't unsee. I have friends that have lost their marriages due to their dependency on porn.

I worked with a guy back when I was in high school. He couldn't believe I had never slept with my girlfriend of two years. He was like, "Don't you want to try that on? I wouldn't buy a pair of shoes without trying them on!" Well, we agreed to disagree. But let me tell you… when you find the right person, all that will work perfectly as it should. You have to trust that the person you are destined for is right for you in every way. Have some faith in the process. I can also tell you that my co-worker lived a jaded existence, where that intimate connection was damaged for him. He was always thinking of who his girlfriend and eventually fiancé had been with previously. He would become self-conscious about the other guys. Were they better than him? I also know of women who have talked about their pre-marriage escapades and how their husbands didn't measure up to those guys. It's a dangerous crack in the foundation of what should be a beautiful home. It is damage. It can and should be avoided.

Even so, we have to be forgiving. Everyone's story is different. We can't predict or guarantee that we will always find what we were hoping for in our spouse's past. If you're an older guy maybe headed into a post-divorce relationship, the idea of a virgin bride is not a part of the equation. In any case, there are a variety of things from upbringing to dire circumstances that can affect these conditions. The important thing is to love unconditionally. Never judge or rule out someone because things were different for them - for whatever reason. Ultimately, we should forgive and forget. Love conquers all.

Chapter Six
ONE PLUS ONE EQUALS ONE

One day you're going to find the right girl. No matter the journey you've both had up to that point, the past is in the past. What matters is what's next.

You may not be at an age where you're thinking about marriage, and this is not a marriage book. That's okay. I'm just trying to give you a vantage point into the future. As I mentioned, I have always been a big picture guy. Even with the girls in elementary school, I was like, "Could I marry her?" In fact, I didn't date one particular girl in high school because of her last name. Kind of shallow I suppose, but I was thinking about how my choices affected me years down the road, and I couldn't imagine our names together in the local newspaper wedding announcements. I won't print it here. Just let your imagination take that one and trust me. It was an awkward combo.

When I was about thirty, I read a book called *Half-Time* by Bob Buford. It was a book intended for middle-aged guys to reassess where they were and to evaluate if they had drifted off course. It was actually good that I read it that early. It gave me a perspective that I probably would not have had. The book addressed the difference between success and significance and helped me evaluate the order of my priorities. Maybe reading a little about marriage now, while gaining some perspective on awareness, will likewise get your mind and heart aimed in the right direction.

We'd all like to think we can be that idyllic prince that saves the princess from the high tower (the one guarded by the fire-breathing dragon). We do fight dragons. Sometimes to get the girl. Sometimes to get the job. Sometimes to keep our sanity. We have to decide when to take up the sword and shield and go after what we want regardless of our fears. There will be dragons that block the light at the end of the tunnel. There will be dragons that make us feel unworthy and defeated. That is why we fight them to show that we have achieved that balance of both prince and protector, and of course, to reach the treasure. One vital component in becoming a man,is finding the right woman.

Genesis 2 states that a man shall leave his mother and father and be joined as one flesh to his wife. It also says you should treat her as you would treat yourself. Ephesians 5:28 states that men should love their wives as their own bodies. No matter where you come from or even what you believe, some things just ring true. You feel it in your soul.

Marriage is not hard. Many people will tell you it is. Making a life and creating a family has to be the best thing I have ever done. I have stated for a while now that if a marriage is hard or ends in divorce, it is because of selfishness. Sometimes the problems seem to be one-sided, but we also see the destructive behavior split right down the middle. I believe when you find the right person you will be enraptured with her presence. You will go out of your way to be with her and to make her happy. Sowing that seed will grow more of the same, and it goes both ways. Paraphrasing Douglas Wilson again: Your life is a musical note; your spouse needs to play a harmony to that note. If you or your spouse tries to force the other to "sing in unison," then each person is not represented in the metaphorical chord. Harmony is always more beautiful than unison.

A
REAL
WOMAN
CAN DO IT ALL BY HERSELF.

A REAL
MAN
WON'T LET
HER.
- UNKNOWN

SHE'S
EVERYTHING
IN MY WHOLE WORLD.
THAT'S MY
FOREVER
GIRL

- JON LANGSTON

One of my best friends got divorced after about fifteen years of marriage. He and his first wife had trouble trying to rekindle that initial flame. Neither one of them would really go out of their way to make a change. It just felt like the candle was out. I always think it's best to try everything to save a marriage. But this one was over. When this friend found a new love out on the West Coast, I could see a dynamic shift in him. He was going out of his way to do anything for her. New love is like that. I get it, and fortunately it lasted. They got married. I told him one day I thought he had finally found his princess - the one for whom he would slay a dragon.

We often hear the word compromise in marriage - that you have to compromise things to get along. In any good relationship, there are compromises, but it's much deeper than that. Two becoming one is a process that never ends, but you will know when it begins. I had been dating my wife for about two months, and we started talking hypothetically about marriage. We wanted to be with each other so badly it was to the point that it was annoying other people. As the next few weeks progressed, we couldn't imagine her finishing two more years of college four hours away. We became engaged and six months later we married on the first anniversary of our first date. She finished college closer to home. It felt like it just had to be that way. There was a love magnet drawing us together, and we couldn't bear to be apart. I have a concept I call The Love Triangle. In this model, I speak about Christ being the North star that keeps us on course, grounded and connected. He is the magnetic mountain that draws us to our faith and together. We can both see the North star from our vantage point, and as we look toward it, standing side-by-side, we create a triangle made of man, woman and God. And God... is love.

If you've had your Forever Girl in mind all along, then just maybe by the time you two meet, you'll have saved yourself for her. And, maybe she for you. That would be awesome! It will bring a greater depth to your relationship immediately. If not, don't beat yourself up. The most important thing, is that you find her.

A couple of years before I met my wife, I heard a guy say, "If you're praying for your wife... might as well be specific." I prayed for a brunette with green eyes. Got it. Results are not guaranteed, but God is faithful.

Have you heard about the Rice Experiment? My understanding is that it came from the basic premise of the book, *The Hidden Messages in Water* by Masaru Emoto. Emoto posits that his experiments revealed that water which was bathed in kind and uplifting words created beautiful snowflake-like crystals of varying unique designs. Water that was berated and subjected to foul language would freeze into broken non-symmetrical shards. Hence, the rice experiment takes three jars of cooked rice and places them into three separate rooms with the same temperature and light. One jar is the control and is basically ignored. The second jar receives ugly and demeaning talk, while the third jar is praised and spoken to with hope and love. At the end of a few weeks, the ignored rice is not looking great. However, the second jar which got all the negative treatment... well, it's turning black. And, the third jar of happy rice... it's white and looks edible. The moral of the story is that our words hold great power. It would appear that merely speaking life or death really does have an impact on the physical world. Words matter at a molecular level. Consider that humans are sixty percent water. When water boils, you can't see straight to see your reflection in it. When the water is calm, there is clarity.

A
MAN
IS TO UNDERSTAND HE DOESN'T
PROTECT
HIS WOMAN
BECAUSE SHE IS WEAK, BUT BECAUSE SHE IS
IMPORTANT.
- UNKNOWN

THE REAL
POWER
OF A MAN

IS THE SIZE OF THE
SMILE
ON THE FACE OF THE
WOMAN
STANDING NEXT TO HIM.

- UNKNOWN

The other day, a woman thought my wife was thirty-five. As of the writing of this book, my wife is fifty. I have told her every day since our relationship began (when she was nineteen) that she is beautiful. It just pops out of my mouth when I look at her. I can't control it. Do I think it matters that I have edified her in this way? Absolutely.

When the right one comes along, tell her she's beautiful every day, and she will be. Tell her you love her every single day, and she will never doubt it. By speaking these truths, the power of your words increases in potency as you prophesy into her future.

Listen to your wife. In the Bible, Wisdom is personified as a woman. You do well to balance your own masculine perspective with that of a virtuous woman. Honor her. And never forget... she is not your mama.

Side Note: Eve gets a bad rap. Adam should have stood in the way of the serpent. Adam should have been watching out for her.

When I was in church youth group as a teenager, one of our Sunday school teachers was a really funny guy. On ski trips, we got to know him a little better, and guess what we learned? His farts were disgusting. We're talking off-the-chart levels of sulfur that required a gas mask to survive. One day, when I found out he would use these infamous stinkers to Dutch Oven his wife, I felt so bad for her. He would emit the gas in bed and pull the sheets up over their heads. It must have been true tor-ture. It still gives me anxiety thinking this actually hap-pened. Unlike another good friend of mine who likes to make it a competition, I have never intentionally farted around my wife. I do know there have been sleep farts.

We all have those. Once in a blue moon, you'll have one wake you up to find your significant other laughing at you. But man... my advice to you: Keep some things a mystery and absolutely no Dutch Ovens.

We were a good nine years into our marriage when my wife was getting frustrated that I was sitting on the couch while she was washing dishes or cleaning up the kitchen. Before we had kids, we ate out so much that there just wasn't much in the sink that needed washing. But by 2001, we had two kids. The pots and pans were now outnumbered by baby bottles and sippy cups. She needed help, and I was sitting on the couch. She finally let fly, "Do you not see what needs to be done in here?" I did not. Now, I do. Dude... wash dishes. As you grow together, this kind of teamwork becomes an unconscious give and take that divides the workload. Moments like this are an investment in your relationship.

One more thought for chapter six... Many times I wish I had not said what I said. Even though my wife loves me and considers me the ultimate catch, I can screw that up quickly with a sharp or thoughtless word. Sometimes it is just blind ignorance, and when things are screwed up, it feels like it will never be fixed. Even though I know she doesn't really hate me, it sure can feel like it. Just the other day, we had a conflict over how to make tea. She was trying to be helpful, but when I pointed out that she did it differently than I would, she took it personally. She felt I was being critical of her, but I really meant nothing by it. It just escalated to the point that you're not sure how you got there. Hopefully, these moments are rare for you. Learn from them. You will get better about not sticking your foot in your mouth. Better. Probably not perfect.

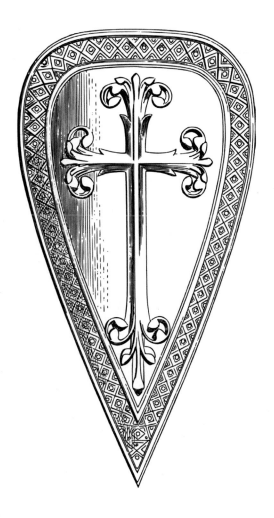

Chapter Seven
A KNIGHT IN SHINING ARMOR

It has been romanticized that women are waiting for their Knight in Shining Armor. Truth be told (and much like today), they weren't all good guys. Hence, the need for the code. The lasting ideals of the chivalrous code are a foundation upon which we twenty-first century "knights" can build. As the kings of our castles and defenders of our families, we stand out front. With sword and shield, we draw the line in the sand between those we love and the destroyer. As with all martial arts, our skill in battle should be employed in defense, not as a course of domination. We should never strike a defenseless opponent, and we should seek peace whenever possible. Proverbs 19:11 relates that the discretion of a man makes him slow to anger, and to overlook a transgression. In life, we will encounter conflict. As I stated earlier, if we can embrace even the hard moments of life, we will truly live. Confrontation creates change, and change can be a really good thing. As we solve problems, there is growth and recognition for our achievement. Battles plant the seed for victory.

Our masculinity needs to be restored. It is not toxic. Some people are toxic, but gender has nothing to do with it. Someone who has had their masculinity white-washed over the years is Jesus Christ. Current trends would have us believe he was all hugs, kisses and miracles all the time. But Jesus was a revolutionary rebel. He did what needed to be done. He challenged the religious system of the day, and he also gave grace to those that didn't deserve it. Jesus made a whip and ran vendors out of the temple, turning over their tables and telling the truth. The truth can get you in trouble, but it is freeing. To paraphrase the great Jordan Peterson: The truth is an adventure, and perhaps, better than playing it safe.

I want to point out that Jesus made a whip. He didn't just grab a stick and run people off. He took the time to craft something that he knew would get the job done.

You may have heard the term "moral compass." It's that still small voice that weighs on you if you are straying into dark territory. There is also an "internal compass," and some of us have better ones than others. This is an invisible version of a real compass that orients us North, South, East and West. My internal compass is pretty good. I have another compass I like to refer to as the "eternal" compass. It's best friends with the moral compass, but it is much more than a guide between right and wrong. In some ways, it's like Captain Jack Sparrow's compass that guides him only to what he truly wants. The eternal compass keeps us mindful of destiny, of the lasting implications of our actions and the impact of our faith. The eternal compass illuminates the future. It is good to take a reading of our compasses daily.

SERVE ALL. LOVE ONE

HONORÉ DE BALZAC

THE ARMOR OF GOD

HELMET OF
SALVATION

BREASTPLATE OF
RIGHTEOUSNESS

BELT OF
TRUTH

SWORD OF THE
SPIRIT

SHIELD OF
FAITH

BOOTS OF PEACE

The Armor of God

10 Finally, my brethren, be strong in the Lord, and in the power of his might. 11 Put on the whole armour of God, that ye may be able to stand against the wiles of the devil. 12 For we wrestle not against flesh and blood, but against principalities, against powers, against the rulers of the darkness of this world, against spiritual wickedness in high places. 13 Wherefore take unto you the whole armour of God, that ye may be able to withstand in the evil day, and having done all, to stand. 14 Stand therefore, having your loins girt about with truth, and having on the breastplate of righteousness; 15 And your feet shod with the preparation of the gospel of peace; 16 Above all, taking the shield of faith, wherewith ye shall be able to quench all the fiery darts of the wicked. 17 And take the helmet of salvation, and the sword of the Spirit, which is the word of God: 18 Praying always with all prayer and supplication in the Spirit, and watching thereunto with all perseverance and supplication for all saints. **Ephesians 6:10-18** / King James Version

Have you ever heard of the Armor of God? It's basically a symbolic thing like putting on your "thinking cap." Just as "putting on your thinking cap" infers that you are taking the time to apply wisdom and deduction to a particular thing, the Armor of God suggests important offensive and defensive ideals to incorporate in our every day lives. This means we get to metaphorically dress like Boba Fett every day!

The armor a knight wore provided protection to their bodies and gave them the weapons needed to advance their cause. Similarly, the armor of God provides us with the accuracy, strength and defenses to live the Chival life. Let's take a look at how it applies.

The Belt of Truth

The first piece of this gnarly outfit is the belt of truth. As you button your pants in the morning, imagine you are securing the belt of truth around your waist. A chivalrous man needs to gird himself in principle. As you trust the truth, lies will deflect off your heart and mind like bullets bounce off of Superman's chest. Truth will never let you (or your pants) down. It will set you free. Plus, the belt of truth is a good place to hang you sword.

The Breastplate of Righteousness

When you put on a cool shirt or your favorite jacket, it gives you some swagger, right? Make sure to keep the breastplate of righteousness in mind along with that strut. The breastplate covers the heart and shields other vital organs. The righteousness of God protects us from the entanglements and accusations of the enemy. We need to put that breastplate on because none of us are righteous in ourselves.

The Boots of Peace

Who doesn't like a nice pair of kicks? A solid pair of shoes gives us confidence and comfort. It's easier to stand firm in a reliable pair of boots. The Bible states that this piece of the armor is the covering of the gospel of peace. Gospel means good news, and in Greek, peace translates as oneness and wholeness. With our feet agile and ready, we can take bold steps out onto the battlefield.

The Shield of Faith

Having "thick skin" helps, but even better... pick up the shield of faith and protect yourself from those fiery darts and vicious strikes. Faith is not from within. It is God's gift to us. As we get to know Him better, our faith grows. As we trust Him, the shield grows in size and strength. It's a supernatural upgrade. Visually, the knight's shield also makes a statement about who he is, where he is from and what kingdom he serves.

The Helmet of Salvation

The crowning piece of any knight's armor is his helmet. It's a pretty big deal. It gives the knight his unique look, and more importantly protects his head. The battlefield of our mind is the place where the angels and demons have their tug of war for our souls. Good and bad ideas emerge from our noggin, so it's vital to wear that helmet. Salvation comes the moment we place our trust in Jesus. It's both instant, and a journey. It's something the knight works out as he endeavors to become the man he is meant to be.

The Sword of the Spirit

Sword-making goes back thousands of years. It's an art form where purpose and design are married into beautiful balance. In the Armor of God, the sword of the Spirit is the Word of God. We can also view our own "voice" in this context and its need to be balanced and wielded with care. The sword is the only part of the armor that is both offensive and defensive, and learning to use it properly comes with practice. Jesus used the sword of the Spirit when rejecting Satan's temptation in the wilderness, by sighting the written Word of God to shut the enemy down with truth.

A Chink in the Armor

The idiom "a chink in one's armor" refers to an area of vulnerability. In the twenty-first century, this would be a crack or gap in a figurative suit of armor that might be an opponent's aim. It's the proverbial weak-link. Similar to the Achilles heel, it could be a fatal flaw that prevents one's success. The chink in the armor is an opening where an attacker can inflict the most damage. Know your weaknesses. Nobody is indestructible.

Prayer

Prayer is not technically part of the armor, however, Paul ends the description of the armor by reminding us of the importance of taking meditative moments of solitude. We need to quiet our minds and listen for answers. Even when we are arrayed in the in the panoply of God, we need to cover it all in prayer - seeking wisdom and direction from the high command.

In the middle ages, chivalry was given its name but it wasn't new. These ideals were framed into a code, but ultimately the hearts of humanity had echoed these truths through the eons before and the ages since. Even though there was corruption then as there is now, the truth of these principles still emerged as a tangible gift for future generations.

Before I go, I would like to come back to the Ten Commandments of Chivalry, and speak to them specifically.

The Ten Commandments of Chivlary

Be Faithful and Have Faith

To be faithful is to be trustworthy and a person of integrity. We should honor the oaths we take before God and man. To have faith is to trust in a higher power. I believe that higher power is the one true God, Yahweh, Father of Jesus Christ and giver of the Holy Spirit. Without faith, I don't know how people make it. In life, there are tough times and without God's shoulder to lean on, I would fall. It's important to acknowledge and trust in our faith at all times, not just when times are tough and not just when times are good. Never bend your convictions to gain anything. What does it profit us if we gain the world, but lose our own soul? Compromising what's for dinner is fine; compromising the guidance of your eternal compass is cataclysmic.

Defend The Weak

There are those that were born into a less-than scenario. There are those that can no longer walk to the kitchen to make dinner without help. There are those whose voices can't yet be heard. Never hesitate to stand up for those in need, and always be ready to lend a hand.

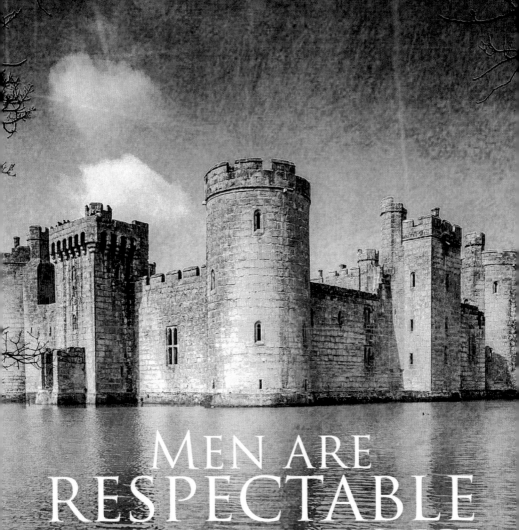

Men are RESPECTABLE only as they respect.

- Ralph Waldo Emerson

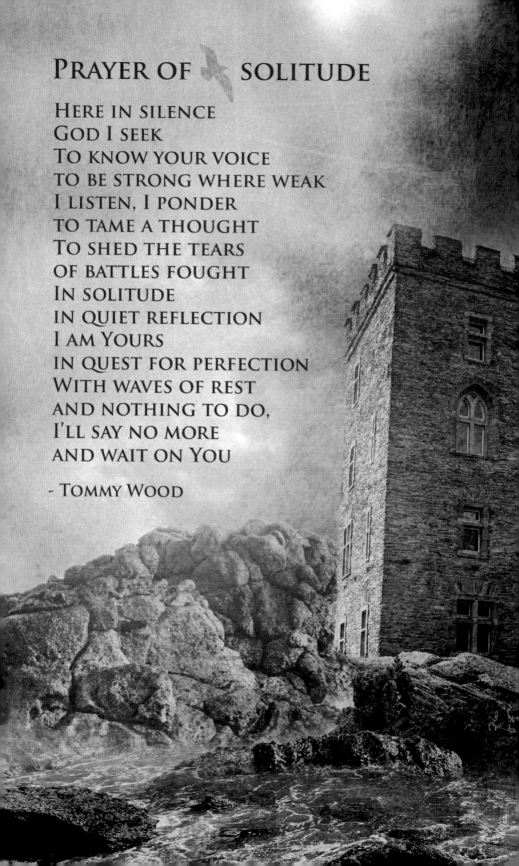

PRAYER OF SOLITUDE

HERE IN SILENCE
GOD I SEEK
TO KNOW YOUR VOICE
TO BE STRONG WHERE WEAK
I LISTEN, I PONDER
TO TAME A THOUGHT
TO SHED THE TEARS
OF BATTLES FOUGHT
IN SOLITUDE
IN QUIET REFLECTION
I AM YOURS
IN QUEST FOR PERFECTION
WITH WAVES OF REST
AND NOTHING TO DO,
I'LL SAY NO MORE
AND WAIT ON YOU

- TOMMY WOOD

Defend Your Country

Many soldiers have gone before us, and millions have paid the ultimate price in defense of their country. We have to be wise and aware of what's happening in our world and in our own land. Sometimes we see the threat from outside our borders. There are plenty of threats from within, as well. In either case, hold the line in defense of the country of your birth. Reject the notions that would bring you to ruin. Defend the ideals that made your nation great.

Take Time for Solitude

In the quiet of a forest, in the silence of your room, on a long drive from home, in the surf by the dune... find a place to ponder. Find a place to think. Find a place to listen, and find a place to dream. The resonate voice inside your heart will speak and guide and often make you laugh. There's a sense of destiny in the quiescent space between where we are and where we are headed. Seek solitude, and wisdom will find you.

Forgive

Forgiveness is the crux of all of our stories, for we are all flawed and born into a broken world. One way we can mend the tears in the fabric of our society is to forgive. I know it can be hard, and some wounds take longer to heal. But if you let unforgiveness fester, you are the one who will pay the heavy price. The poison of that resentment leaks into your blood, and can take a physical toll on your health. Let go, and let God have it. Some say they can forgive but not forget. Honestly, that might be the way to do it. But as with everything else, try to achieve the pinnacle. Try to forgive... and forget.

Work Hard

My dad always said there was a sense of satisfaction in a good day's work, no matter what the job was. There is truth to that. Whether it's a day working in the yard, managing a company's IT or even delivering pizza, we should do that job to our best ability. We do have to pay the bills after all. Just don't let a job, take you away from your life's work. Hopefully, at some point, your career and your passions are one and the same. Jordan Peterson said, "Work as hard as you can on at least one thing, and see what happens." Whether it be writing a book, writing a song, painting a picture or designing a brand new logo for an upstart business, I love to be working in my creative space. Your wheelhouse might be different from mine. Everyone has their own ship to sail. Vision is vital to keeping the light of hope in your eyes, and your course set on the horizon.

Be Patient. Respect Others

Patience is the capacity to accept delay, trouble, or suffering without getting angry. You've probably heard that patience is a virtue. It is. A virtue is defined as "behavior showing high moral standards," so I would pose that patience is at the core of what it means to be chivalrous. When we think of the word "respect," I think we think we know what it means, but how long has it been since we've read the definition? I felt the best way to write about respect here is to merely define it. Respect is a "feeling of deep admiration for someone or something elicited by their abilities, qualities or achievements." We might be even more familiar with the idea of understanding respect defined as esteem or regard for the feelings, wishes, rights or traditions of others. My suggestion is to read that again slowly and consider where in your life you might need to show a little more respect.

We have to LOOK THE BEAST IN THE MOUTH, AND DESPITE ITS BLOODY TEETH AND FIERY BREATH, DEFEND WHAT IS RIGHT AND TRUE.

- TOMMY WOOD

YOUR
REPETITION
BECOMES YOUR
REPUTATION.
- KRIS VALATON

Be Honest. Never Lie

Being honest isn't just about not lying. Being honest is about communicating with sincere transparency. It's about saying what you mean, and meaning what you say. The Bible says let your yes be yes, and your no be no. Honesty is being the same person in public, as you are alone in your room. Honesty is not just what we say, it's what we do.

Be Generous and Gracious

I enjoy being generous. It's not just about money and donations. We can be generous with our time, our resources, our skills and our gifts. My parents were generous with all the above. My mom served in the Meals on Wheels program, and my dad was known to sell someone his car for a dollar if he was about to buy a new one. My good friend and author Chuck Reaves relates his mantra to "Teach Others". Passing on our knowledge and experience to the next generation is a benevolent time-saving contribution. Being gracious is to be courteous and kind. I think it's also to be thankful. We can get so caught up with what we want and not content with what we have. Thankfulness sows a seed that produces joy.

Be Courageous - Champion of Right and Good

Being truly courageous can actually cost us. Sometimes the courageous thing to do is not the popular thing. When we go against the grain, it can actually anger people that we have the boldness to do what they won't do. Whether you're challenged to perform some heroic act, or tasked to do something noble that goes against the grain, do it with the confidence of a champion who fights for what is right and good. Truth is on your side, and history tends to shine a favorable light on the courageous.

I realize what I have laid out in this book sets a high bar. Many will find aspects of my philosophy unreasonable and unrealistic for the modern world. Just as Chivalry raised a lofty standard, so to does CHIVAL provide a precise mark. Will we miss? Sure. Can we incrementally improve as we set our sights on that goal? Absolutely.

The glimmer of our armor reflects to the four corners of the earth. Sunlight on the steel of our word shines forever. Legacy is born through diligence and time. What we do today echoes throughout eternity. A chivalrous man fights the good fight with a warrior-poet ethos and a heart of gold. After his journey, the hero returns with the healing elixir discovered on his quest. He adores those entrusted to him and builds a house of love around them. The knight in shining armor defends and leads. He instills faith, hope and love into his flock. He is the shield between the adversary and his brood.

It starts now, and it starts with you.

Today is the seed for tomorrow.

Slay the dragons.

Be Chival.

Made in the USA
Columbia, SC
01 December 2022

72446424R00053